The Story (
A Life Lived (

Anne Lyons PBVM

The Icon of Nano Nagle by Desmond Kyne

First published in 2021 by Messenger Publications

ISBN: 9781788123228

Cover photograph of Nano Nagle statue at Ballygriffin
© Liam O'Connell SJ

Scripture quotations are from several versions, including the New
Revised Standard Version which is used by permission.
All rights reserved worldwide.

Designed by Messenger Publications Design Department
Typeset in Sabon LT Pro and Prague Std
Printed by W & G Baird

Messenger Publications,
37 Leeson Place, Dublin D02 E5V0, Ireland
www.messenger.ie

CONTENTS

TIMELINE OF THE LIFE OF NANO NAGLE

1695	Act of Education is passed, forbidding Irish Catholics from seeking education abroad.
1718	Nano Nagle is born in Ballygriffin, Co. Cork.
1728	Beginning of her first stay in France.
1746	Death of her father, Garret. Nano returns to Ireland.
1746–48	Death of Nano's mother, Ann (Mathews), and of her sister, Ann Nagle. Nano returns to France briefly before moving to Cork to live with her brother Joseph.
1754	Nano opens her first school in Cove Lane, Cork city.
1757	Death of her uncle and benefactor, Joseph Nagle.
1769	Nano has opened a total of 7 schools in Cork city.
1771	Nano brings four Ursuline sisters to Ireland to aid her in her work, but due to the ecclesiastical law of enclosure they are unable to travel throughout Cork city.
1775–77	Nano Nagle with three companions founds the Presentation Sisters. They will support her vision and continue her work.
1784	Death of Nano on 26 April and burial in Cork.

PREFACE

This booklet has one purpose: to share essential brushstrokes of the graced life story of the Venerable Nano Nagle, whose life stands as a witness to the power of the Holy Spirit at work in one individual. Of special significance in our day is the fact that she lived the greater part of her life as a laywoman who championed the cause of right – a bearer of light to a darkened world.

Nano is not some unreachable human being. She can be a good companion to us. She was not flawless. She knew times of impatience, anger, frustrations, and vexations. She could be firm, stubborn, demanding of herself and of her infant community. Her life of excessive asceticism coupled with endless days of apostolic engagement proved too demanding for some of her followers. She experienced the daily toil of existence with its successes and failures but matched it with deep contemplative prayer. An earthenware vessel, her strength lay in the Lord, and she found in him the courage and spiritual power she needed to rise again and again and continue on her pilgrim journey, the lamp of her life forever aglow with God's love.

> 'Nano Nagle, a woman ablaze with God, you daily walked the razor's edge of life, witnessing to the divine conspiracy of love. Awaken within us the fire of loving service so that like you we may continue to go one pace beyond.'

CHAPTER ONE
A WOMAN ABLAZE WITH GOD

Ballygriffin, Co. Cork, Nano's Birthplace

In his Easter 2020 message, Pope Francis urged humankind to be 'a contagion of hope' and spoke of people being 'windows of hope', 'witnesses to the Paschal event' in a darkened and suffering world. He added that what humankind most needed were people who would be 'gateways of hope and transformation'. Pope Francis could have been speaking of Nano Nagle, because her story reveals a woman whose passion and zeal radically changed the lives of the poor in her native city and country, and which, through the Congregation she founded, touched the wider world.

Nano was born in Ballygriffin, Co. Cork, in 1718. Her family circumstances guaranteed her a life of security, wealth and privilege. For most Irish people, however, the eighteenth century was a bleak and dark period of Irish history. A death-dealing contagion was steadily wreaking its devastating consequences on the lives of most Catholics, who were dominated by repressive and unjust English laws; these were rightly called 'penal laws' because of their punishing intent. They brought denial of education, of ownership of property and of freedom of religious worship. They severely diminished the quality of life for all Irish Catholics but particularly for the poor.

Breaches of the Penal Laws resulted in certain punishment – either prison, the gallows or deportation and life-long exile from native land and loved ones. In reference to the Penal Laws, Edmund Burke, the renowned orator and a contemporary relative of Nano, said, 'It was a machine of wise and elaborate contrivance and as well fitted for the oppression, impoverishment and degradation of people and the debasement in them of human nature itself, as ever proceeded from the perverted ingenuity of man'.

It was against this sombre and dark landscape that Nano Nagle emerged, risking her life to bring glimmers of light to the destitute. We will explore the events that occasioned her radical awakening and conversion, but for now, suffice to say that the magnitude of her daring, pioneering and courageous achievement against the system's might cannot be overestimated.

She opened what Pope Francis termed 'windows of hope'. Daring to do what no one else at that time would risk, she opened 'gateways of transformation' for countless people. In championing the cause of the poor, she became a voice for the voiceless and a hope for the hopeless. The Nagle family motto, *Non vox sed votum*, 'Not words but deeds', leapt from the family plaque and was writ boldly on the canvas of her life.

DIVINE ALLUREMENT

As Nano's journey unfolds, it will be revealed how the steady and alluring presence of God became known to her through the most ordinary of events of her life. Her response was one of wholehearted surrender to the call of the gospel and to walking the path of radical discipleship. Abandoning a life of privilege, position and wealth, she moved to align herself to live and work in her beloved city of Cork, in solidarity with those made destitute. Driven by a burning passion to help Christ's marginalised, she dared not only to dream a better life for them but to make this impossible dream a lived reality. This was the great miracle of her life. At a time when the role of women in shaping society was severely restricted, she lived on the razor's edge, a woman fearless before a tyrannical world.

A SEED GROWING

When she commenced her life's work in 1754 for the poor of Cork, Nano adopted a humble, quiet, sometimes hidden manner. Aware of the political reality of the times she did what she could to avoid drawing the unwelcome attention of the authorities. Like the seed Jesus spoke about in the gospel, her work grew unobtrusively but steadily and continues to this day to yield a rich harvest throughout the world. The crystal-clear testimony, the extraordinary legacy and the dynamic spirituality of Nano cannot be disputed. In the words of author Edwina Gately:

You were not normal, Nano.
You were possessed and driven by God, calling you
  into a Great Love-Conspiracy
to make a difference in a hurting world,
leaving all of us timid and doubting souls with a
  legacy of miracles
born and forged from your courage, determination
  and deep, hidden suffering.

Here was a woman of deep mystical heart, a great lover

of God's poor, a fearless woman who stood unprotected before the beckoning voice of her God. Watch her as she resolutely steps away from a life of ease and wealth and finds her Divine Lover in the guise of the needy and the outcast.

'GO TO THE POOR: THEY WILL TEACH YOU!'

While she was an escort of grace to the poor, they in turn became escorts of grace to her. By being in communion with them and contemplating their misery, the pores of her comfortable existence were gradually opened. The shackles of glitz, glamour and comfort steadily unravelled. Radical empathy and deep compassion for the needy were birthed in her as she championed them and challenged the oppressive system that denied the fundamental right of Irish people to Catholic education.

Nano spent long hours daily in prayer contemplating the life of Jesus. Her entire life was rooted in his life and mission: 'to bring Good News to the poor, to set prisoners free, to give sight to the blind, and to usher in a time of liberation' (Luke 4:18). Willingly led by the Holy Spirit, Nano set about her mission of liberation and transformation. Like the prophet Jeremiah, a fire burned in her bones (see Jeremiah 20:9).

LED BY A LANTERN FLAME

Nano Nagle believed that the right to education was the prerogative of all, not just of the privileged. Long before Thomas Davis's slogan 'Educate that you may be free!' rang out across Ireland she knew that education was the key to the empowerment, transformation and liberation of her people. She grieved their poverty, their rampant ignorance and their lack of faith, the consequence of over a century of bondage. She felt that she must act! And so it was that in 1754, in the face of the filth and poverty she saw around her, she began the dangerous project of setting up what she called 'her little schools'.

Driven only by love, Nano gathered around her the children from the hovels of Cork. Daily she trudged to her seven schools to teach her pupils. And each evening after her long day's work Nano could be seen, with lantern lit, moving contemplatively through the dangerous and winding streets of Cork city. The poor were not invisible to her as they were to so many of her class; in their faces she discerned the face of Jesus Christ: 'I was hungry, thirsty, lonely, imprisoned ... and you visited me' (Matthew 25:36). She shone her lantern light of faith, hope and loving service into their lives. It was the fire of divine love burning within her heart that enabled her to endure in hope the disappointments, rejection and failure that she encountered. It has been said that the saints are case studies in the performance of hope: they accompany us in our struggles. Nano's life is surely a living testament to the virtue of enduring Christian hope.

A GLOBAL VISION OF LOVING SERVICE

From 1754 to 1771 Nano Nagle sought as a lone layperson to serve the poor through her schools. When at fifty-seven she was growing frailer in health, she found herself longing to ensure that her legacy would endure. Her hopes for the continuity of her work focused on the Ursuline Sisters, whom she brought from France to Ireland in 1771. This congregation had been founded in Italy in 1535. However due to the rule of enclosure – a long standing ecclesiastical restriction on religious women from moving about freely – the Ursulines could not leave their convents to work with Nano in her schools. One can only imagine the great disappointment this prohibition caused her.

Her undaunted passion and vision drew the attention of three other women who became her companions, and on Christmas Eve 1775, together with her little band, she founded the religious congregation that is now known as The Presentation Sisters of the Blessed Virgin Mary.

Mary of the Presentation

This was the first such religious foundation in Ireland for many centuries, and it led to many more, as we shall see. Nano Nagle thus occupies a unique place in Irish history. Out of the long night of darkness occasioned by the Penal Laws, this small and frail woman gave her all, like the widow in the gospel who presented her life's goods to God and was blessed for her generosity (see Luke 21:1–4). In 2000, she was voted Irish Woman of the Millennium in recognition of her importance as a pioneer of female education in Ireland. In 2005 she was voted by radio poll to be Ireland's greatest ever woman. She inspired Blessed Edmund Ignatius Rice to found the Christian Brothers in 1802 and bring education to poor boys in Ireland and beyond.

I quote one of her biographers, Sr Raphael Consedine: 'Nano Nagle, spirit-led, Spirit strengthened, was wholly woman in her response to God's action in her life. She lived fully the essence of womanhood – to be life-bearer, life-nurturer among her people. She did not spend her energies on anger or on violence in response to injustice, nor did she let herself be paralysed by the magnitude of the problems around her. Accepting the suffering which her decisions entailed, she gave to others the gift of life and of a future'.

NANO NAGLE IS ALIVE!

She had expressed her global vision from the very beginning: 'If I could be of service in saving souls in any part of the world, I would willingly do all in my power.' Today a world-wide network of sisters, colleagues, associates, friends of Nano – all the Presentation Family – continue to collaborate in beaming the lantern flame of hope and transformation into the lives of the needy, across geographical, political and cultural borders. Her pioneering spirit is alive and well, as the following incident shows.

The year was 2006 and I had returned to work with our sisters in Pakistan. The date was 21 November, our titular feast, which is celebrated worldwide by the Presentation Family. I was invited to our school in Jhelum, where the students and teachers had prepared a wonderful programme and I found myself seated beside a high-ranking Pakistani Army official, the chief guest. At the conclusion of the programme, accompanied by his aide-de-camp, he left my side and marched to the podium. The eyes of more than a thousand young students were focused on him, and the words that flowed from his mouth were riveting. He shared with us that until that afternoon he had never heard of Nano Nagle. Then, striking the podium with passion, and with a booming voice, he proclaimed to his awestruck audience, 'Nano Nagle is not dead: Nano Nagle is alive. She is here in this school and in this place'. He concluded with the challenging words: 'What we need, what the world needs is more Nano's!' As we shall see, happily his call has borne fruit in Pakistan as well as elsewhere.

VENERABLE NANO

The recognition of Nano's life of heroic virtue, deep faith, loving service and radical commitment to those made poor was validated on 31 October 2013, when Pope Francis named her Venerable, a further step on the path towards her canonisation (she was declared 'Servant of God' in 1994). Nano Nagle takes her place among those called and chosen to be witnesses to a life of love and stands now as an icon of God's love for our world. To borrow the words of Pope Francis with which we began, Nano continues to be 'a contagion of hope', 'a gateway for transformation' against the unjust systems that continue to hold sway in our world today. Her dying words to the small circle of companions gathered around her deathbed on 26 April 1784 were: 'Love one another as you have hitherto done'.

FOR PONDERING

Another biographer, Salvador Fink, writes of Nano Nagle in these words: 'Meet a woman whose love was stronger than the viciousness, greed, and violence that swamped her city and nation. She was a woman of unbounded compassion, deep contemplation, indomitable courage, radical creativity, native shrewdness, and indefatigable zeal for her faith. Challenging the brutal power of her people's oppression she spent her life on the "razor's edge of danger"'.

CHAPTER 2
NANO'S FORMATIVE YEARS

In 1718, in the townland of Ballygriffin, near Mallow, Co. Cork, a baby girl was born to Garret Nagle and Ann Mathew. She was their first-born child and the eldest of seven children – five girls and two boys. Her baptismal name was Honora, but she was known to her parents, family and contemporaries as Nano.

The Nagles were a society family with wealth and land at their disposal so Nano's early environment was one of safety, comfort and privilege. She was fortunate to live a happy childhood in the ancestral surrounding of Ballygriffin, a place enveloped by the beauty of nature in its manifold expressions: the spacious and lush greenness of the surrounding countryside, the Nagle Mountains and the flowing water of the Blackwater River.

She has been described as a vivacious, lively, wilful and spirited young girl. However, her free-spirited nature was a cause of distress to her mother: she had a love of risk, climbing trees, riding ponies, playing in the nearby river. Nano's father, even at this early stage, seems to have sensed something deeper in his beloved daughter. His exclamation has survived the passage of three centuries: 'Nano will be a saint yet'. What must he think now that she bears the title 'Venerable Nano'!

Despite the restrictive measures of the Penal Laws which had come into force about 1700, her parents provided her with every available opportunity to nurture and develop both her Catholic faith and her education. Nano was no doubt familiar with the secret gatherings of people at the local Mass Rocks, hidden deep in the surrounding valleys, where people risked their lives to worship and to strengthen their weary spirits.

'IT TAKES A FAMILY'

The current interest in genealogy sometimes brings surprising revelations to the researcher. A brief glimpse at the gallery of Nano's maternal and paternal ancestors reveals strong hints of how their lives and qualities would later emerge in her life and actions.

Nano's maternal great-great-grandmother was an Elizabeth Poyntz, a Catholic Englishwoman who in the early 1600s had married Thomas Butler, Viscount of Thurles, but was widowed after his untimely death by drowning. She subsequently married George Mathew of Raydr, Wales. Elizabeth was an intrepid defender of the faith and was known for her protection of priests who were being hunted by the authorities. She paid the price: her lands were confiscated when two Inquisitions in 1656 asserted that she had been assisting the Catholic forces with arms and men. She and her son James were reinstated to their lands in 1660 when Charles II ascended the throne. An interesting marginal note is that this devout Englishwoman was to become the common ancestress, through her Butler children, of Prince Charles and the late Princess Diana.

A history of Thurles includes the following data. 'The Mathew line produced the saintly foundress of the Presentation Order of Nuns, Nano Nagle (daughter of Anne Mathew of Anfield), and the great nineteenth century Apostle of Temperance, Father Theobald Mathew. Lady Thurles' contemporary and cousin, Mary Poyntz, was cofounder with Mary Ward of the Institutes of the

Blessed Virgin Mary'.

On the Nagle side Nano's ancestors were equally daring in defying the Penal Laws, providing a place of worship for the people. Nano's own parents carried this deep devotion and fidelity to the faith. One person particularly significant in Nano's history was her Uncle Joseph, her father's brother. He was a barrister in Cork, forbidden under the Penal Laws to practise, and yet 'the most feared by the authorities of any Catholic in the realm'. When Nano in the 1750s dared to begin her little schools in secret, flaunting these laws, he would prove to be her staunchest ally.

Uncle Joseph

Nano received her early education, partly under the tutelage of a wandering schoolmaster, Master O'Halloran, at a hedge school in the crumbling ruins of Monanimy Castle, once the home of her forebears. As a young child she was shielded from many of the harsh realities of life by a web of loving family relationships and grew up with an awareness of being deeply cared for and provided for by a provident God who loved her dearly. Such were the tender years of childhood from 1718 to 1728.

YOUNG WOMAN IN PARIS

Nano would have been aware that a day would come when like many other children of well-to-do families of the eighteenth century she would be smuggled out of Ireland to complete her education. So it was that for almost twenty years from 1728 until 1746 this Irish girl completed her education and then enjoyed society life in Paris. Let's imagine what this passage of her life must have been for her. What was it like for her to be torn from her familiar surroundings, exiled from her parents and borne across the sea to a new country? What did she learn as she listened to her relatives speak of their native land? Alongside the fears, sadness and loneliness of uprooting, was there excitement as she looked forward to being with her cousins in this new land? Nano would have had many adjustments to make regarding culture, language, and Church.

EDUCATION AND SOCIETY LIFE

We cannot say for certain which schools she attended; perhaps firstly at the Benedictine Abbey at Ypres in Belgium. Then, since France carried none of the religious restrictions of her own land, spiritual horizons began to open up to her in a land where the Church held an honoured place. Maybe she found God in the ancient cathedrals of Paris where solemn liturgies were openly celebrated?

Again, we might wonder how the Parisian life of leisure impacted on her. Did she hear God's voice break through in the leisurely days and the soirées that continued into the early morning hours? While there is much that we do not know about Nano, we do know for certain that she enjoyed the carefree life of Paris in the company of her younger sister Ann, whom she held in great regard.

We know of her own self-condemnation in her later years, when she shared that she was 'a lover of the world, of dress and of vanity'. The *Annals* of South Presentation Convent, Cork, record the words of Mother Aloysius Moylan, who knew Nano well. 'You have heard, *sans doute*, that she had been fond of the world when young, enjoyed its amusements, and when obliged to return from France to Ireland, regretting its various enjoyments, she felt deprived of everything pleasant or desirable, yet I do not believe that she neglected the Main Point.'

AN EARLY MORNING ENCOUNTER

In her twenties, Nano experienced a series of disorienting events which were to shock her to her very depths and lead to a radical turn-about from the small and privileged world in which she had been safely cocooned. She found herself propelled without warning into a world of injustice and discrimination.

She must herself have narrated the following moment of initial awakening. She and her companions were being driven home in the early hours of the morning after another night of dance, music and fun. As she sat in her carriage, her attention was drawn to a small group of people huddled at the doors of an unopened Church. It struck her keenly that they were waiting to give the first fruits of their day to God through the Mass, while she was wasting away the precious gift of her young life. This incident occasioned in her some inner stirrings and reflection on the meaning of her life; but was not enough as yet to radically alter her lifestyle. More shocks would be needed to reinforce the impact of that early morning incident and alert her to the whisper of God in the guise of the poor.

GOD IN A MISSING ROLL OF SILK

It has been said that holiness comes wrapped in the ordinary. In 1746 Nano and Ann, still in France, received the sad news of the death of their father, Garret. This occasioned their return to Ireland, and they went to live with their widowed mother in Dublin. Dublin was a sharp contrast to the affluent and carefree environment of Paris to which she had grown so accustomed. There she had been largely shielded from the face of poverty but here it was all about her, with its accompanying sickness, disease,

Penal Laws:
Hanging noose

famine and ignorance. The effects of the Penal Laws were still in evidence especially among the poor and did not end until Catholic Emancipation in 1829.

Prior to her return, Nano had bought a roll of silk. With her mind focused on fashion she had intended to use it to enlarge her already extensive wardrobe: it symbolised a way of life to which she had grown accustomed during her Parisian years. She was aware that, in time, invitations would come her way to attend society evenings in Dublin. One such invitation soon arrived: the silk would serve its intended purpose. However, it was nowhere to be found.

Ann had seen with different eyes the abject poverty of their near neighbours in Dublin. Her response to such poverty was to act: she had sold the silk to alleviate their suffering. Once again, but at a more radical level, God had turned up, this time disguised in a roll of silk. Ann's life of piety and devotion found concrete manifestation in her service to the poor, and her example would deeply influence Nano. Ann was a conduit of grace to her, and became her teacher, bringing her to visit the homes of the poor.

NANO THE PILGRIM

Between 1746 and 1748 came two further blows: the death of her mother and her well-loved sister, Ann. As a woman of rank it was not acceptable at that time for her to continue to live alone in Dublin in the absence of her mother and of Ann. Reeling with grief she returned to the solace and familiarity of her beloved homestead, Ballygriffin. There she lived in the company of her brother David and his new bride, Mary. The memories of childhood days would, it was hoped, bring some solace and healing balm to her grieving heart.

However, instead of peace and solace, her return to Ballygriffin occasioned a further crisis. She passed her time there taking an interest in the family estate, visiting the homes of the poor nearby and offering some education to the children. It was here that she discovered that what they had of religion had degenerated into superstition. Nano was both appalled and overwhelmed by the lack of faith, the pervasive squalor and the ignorance. Once again she turned to the Lord: What was she to do? What was God asking of her?

FRANCE

The *Presentation Annals* reveal her response: 'it was then that she resolved that had she thousands she would dedicate them to the poor. But no prospect of that kind opening, she retired to a convent in France'. Tucked away in these terse words is her enduring and burning passion for the poor. But not having the means to serve them directly, she took what seemed to her the best means of serving them, through at life of prayer. So, she returned to France to live as a religious. Was she in a right disposition at the time to make such a pivotal and life-altering decision? Who can say?

Little is known of this second period of time that Nano spent in France. But wherever her convent was, she did not enjoy inner peace. Instead, she experienced inner turmoil and disturbance, and was plagued by dreams and haunted by the memories of the faces of the poor. In both Ballygriffin and Cork she had witnessed their horrendous living circumstances: filth, disease, deprivation, alongside widespread lawlessness. All this preyed upon her, leaving her bereft of any consolation. Her efforts to resolve this inner disturbance proved in vain. She asked herself, 'What is God up to?' Hadn't she given up everything in coming to France to dedicate herself to a life of prayer?

CORK

According to the *Ursuline Annals*, Nano 'laid open her mind to a learned son of St Ignatius'. This unnamed Jesuit must have sifted sensitively through the inner turmoil and the sharp struggle she was experiencing, and with a clarity and directness he helped her to identify God's call. She must return to Ireland and harness the passion for justice which burned within her, by setting up schools for the deprived children of Cork city who so occupied her heart.

However, Nano's response to this advice didn't come without further wrestling with God. Dr Coppinger, her first biographer, tells us that 'she replied, she argued, she remonstrated' but the *Annals* state the outcome: 'After understanding there the will of heaven, she returned to Ireland'.

FOR PONDERING

Nano herself, in 1769, wrote about that life-changing moment to Miss Eleanor Fitzsimons, 'Nothing would have made me come home but the decision of the clergyman that I would run a great risk of salvation if I did not follow the invitation'. She was then about thirty years of age.

Where have I wrestled with God in my life?

CHAPTER 3
NANO'S CONVERSION

We have been sketching out some key moments in Nano's conversion. Let us pause for a moment to look more closely at this experience of conversion. It is an awakening to the true meaning of life, becoming uncoiled from self-absorption, so as to point one's life-compass in an entirely new direction – towards encounter with the gospel Christ.

The gospels offer many encounters in which Jesus opened eyes to new insight, unblocked ears to hear more deeply and compassionately, loosened tongues to witness to God's activity, and brought freedom from enslaving shackles. Author Richard Rohr writes that 'None of us grows into our spiritual maturity completely of our own accord, or by a totally free choice. We are led there by Mystery...what people rightly call grace'. The scriptures are wrapped around the repeated call to love. It is the final legacy of Jesus to his chosen ones: 'This is my command, that you love one another' (John 15:12, 17). Jesus knows full well, however, that we find it difficult to live out a life of unrestricted love. It would cost not less than everything. Jesuit Daniel Berrigan puts it starkly: 'if you are going to follow Jesus, you better look good on a Cross'. While it is true that most of us desire to live in this unrestricted mode, our illusory self fiercely resists being toppled from its pedestal. No surprise that Jesus would say that it is a hard road and a narrow path, and that few find it (see Matthew 7:14).

MILESTONES OF GRACE

Nano experienced in the depth of her being such milestones of grace. If we were to speak with her today, I imagine she would happily share with us how the scales gradually fell from her eyes through the events in which God managed to get through to her. We can hear her voice: 'Always the poor! Their voices and faces haunted me. They were God's instruments of saving grace. Through them, I was finally won over to what was previously shocking, abhorrent and unpalatable'.

A NEW BEING

A person captivated by God becomes what St Paul describes as a new being, a new creation (see 2 Corinthians 5:17). The writings of the saints offer us a gallery of women and men, who when seized by divine love, symbolise their commitment to a transformed way of living by some external symbol of renunciation. So, St Francis of Assisi abandons his life of wealth for a life of simplicity and poverty; St Clare of Assisi shuns her luxurious upbringing to embrace a life of poverty and piety. St Ignatius of Loyola spends an entire night in vigil before the image of Our Lady of Monserrat and the next day, dressed in pilgrim garb gives his fine clothes to a startled beggar.

Nano did no less. She traded in her silken gowns for a simple black one, unadorned. She exchanged her fancy lace bonnet for a plain hat, and her previous flowing cloak no longer has the swish of silk, but is replaced by a black plain cloak with a hood to shield her somewhat from inclement weather.

DANCE OF INTIMACY

Many years ago, the writer Joyce Rupp wrote of the Dance of Intimacy in which the one desire of the Lord of the Dance is to sweep out the chambers of our hearts. When the clogged areas are cleared our love will then flow freely towards a world in need of justice, truth and compassion.

In Paris Nano had happily danced away the hours of her young womanhood in the company of distinguished partners. After a series of 'interruptions' she yielded herself into the arms of the Lord of the Dance who led her from uncertainty into taking decisive steps towards a new endeavour in the service of his Kingdom. The music of justice, compassion, care and concern for a suffering world steadily took hold of her.

History offers us examples of notable figures who entered into this dance of intimacy with the Lord and his beloved poor. Mother Teresa and Dorothy Day, both women from the twentieth century, but from diverse backgrounds and different countries, yielded to the Jesus of the gospels. Their decisive option for the poor cost them not less than everything. Others were brought face to face with death by assassination. One thinks of Oscar Romero, of the Jesuits in El Salvador and most recently of Clement Shahbaz Bhatti, the only Christian member of Pakistan's National Assembly, who worked tirelessly on behalf of the country's minorities and was assassinated on 2 March 2011.

PAYING ATTENTION

For Nano Nagle the journey home from the Parisian ball, the roll of silk and the burden of loss, grief, and death were life-changing events, but only because she paid attention.

The poet Mary Oliver wrote, 'To pay attention, this is our endless and proper work' and this became Nano's lifelong occupation. To what did she give such attention? I imagine her walking the narrow and winding lanes of Cork, in later years aided by a walking stick. I see her gaze on the faces of the ignorant children, the despised prostitutes, the elderly and unwanted sick hidden from view in disease-ridden hovels. Her gaze was attentive, fuelled by the ever-burning question in her heart: 'What ought I do for them?' Slowly the path had unfolded before her. She surrendered: she would pour out her one wild precious life on the poor!

As this relationship with the Lord matured no one could fail to notice the radical change in her. Her elite and comfortable circle of family and friends found themselves disturbed and challenged, while the disenfranchised found a companion, a champion and a voice that would not be silenced.

Through her pioneering decisions and actions a profile of Nano's character comes into bold relief: a woman of faith, tenacity, courage and conviction; a woman discreet, practical and prudent. Her entire life is now rooted in her one concern: 'the will of the Almighty' revealed in the faces of the poor. This vision guided her every decision and sustained her.

FOR PONDERING

'None of us grows into our spiritual maturity completely of our own accord, or by a totally free choice. We are led there by Mystery ... what people rightly call grace.' (Richard Rohr)

Have I a sense of being won over to God?

CHAPTER 4
NANO'S FIRST SCHOOLS

On her return to Ireland from her second time in France, Nano accepted the invitation to live with her sister-in-law Frances and her brother Joseph in Cork City. Armed only with courage and daring, she strides forward on a new and radical path and she takes the most radical and life-altering decision of her life. She would establish schools for the poor Catholic children of Cork.

As Sr Raphael Considine wrote, 'The spiralling energies of God defy containment', and they coursed through every fibre of her being. Filled with zeal and passion she set about dismantling the unjust barriers to Catholic education that held people enslaved in ignorance and rampant poverty. Her schools would be the key to bring this injustice to an end.

Firm in her trust that 'the Almighty is all-sufficient' and that he 'makes use of the weakest means to bring about his work', she forged ahead with a confidence that 'God is all we need; His Divine Hand will always support us.'

A HUMBLE COTTAGE

We can see that Nano was steadily being won over by God to what was humanly unpalatable. Drawn into a deep contemplative relationship with God alongside a profound consciousness of the poor, she began to slip away from the familiar and comfortable world of position and privilege towards the peripheries of society. She took to searching out the children who were in dire need of education and, leaving the grandeur of her brother and sister-in-law's Cork townhouse, she found a humble cottage among the poor in Cove Lane.

From that time forward, her actions and decisions had but one focus: she consciously chose to live in solidarity and communion with the poor and commanded her followers to do likewise: 'Spend yourselves for the poor.'

EDUCATIONAL LANDSCAPE OF CORK

A sketch of the educational landscape of Cork at this time will contextualise her project for the education of the poor. In the 1750s the only access to education for poor children in Cork was through a Charity School and it was for boys only. It provided English education for Protestant boys and 'popish natives' but the intention was to proselytise. Apart from that there were some Charter Schools around the county. However, accounts of these schools reveal that they left a great deal to be desired: reports state that 'the children were very dirty, their clothes in rags ... beds were filthy and the windows of every room were broken'. Nano would have heard accounts of these schools when she was living with Joseph and Frances.

Poor children, Cork

In 1754 she took the daring step to be an educator. She believed in the power of education to transform lives: now she had to make that belief concrete and practical. The *Petite École* Movement begun in France in the eighteenth century offered free education and taught trades, literacy, numeracy and faith. Nano was influenced by this and drew

Mud cabin

on it in the setting up of her own schools.

In 1754 she identified a suitable area in Cove Lane, rented a mud cabin with earthen floors and opened her first school. In his biography of Nano Nagle, Bishop Coppinger describes how she was absolutely terrified by the wickedness of the children. Yet she faced down this fear, set herself to the task of teaching them to read and write, and placed great emphasis on instructing them in their faith.

NOT WORDS, BUT DEEDS

The Nagle motto shimmers through the following personal account of this momentous and daring decision – 'I kept my design a profound secret, as I knew, if it were spoken of, I should meet with opposition on every side, particularly from my immediate family as in all appearance they could suffer from it. My confessor was the only person I told of it; and as I could not appear in the affair, I sent my maid to get a good mistress and to take in thirty poor girls. When this little school was settled I used to steal there in the morning: my brother thought I was at the chapel'. Soon she would have two more schools for girls nearby in Cove Lane. The numbers rapidly grew. Nano, knowing well that her brother Joseph would not approve of this dangerous enterprise, kept her plans a secret. Her mode of proceeding seems to have been, act first, tell later!

When Joseph discovered what was afoot some months later, he flew into a rage. Surely, he asked, Nano must have realised the gravity of her actions, the danger in which she was placing not just herself but also her immediate and extended family? Had she not considered the grave retribution that would visit the Nagle families should this new endeavour be discovered? Against such questioning and caution, Nano remained resolute and firm. Nothing would dissuade her or deflect her mission. Eventually she succeeded in changing the hearts of her family: Joseph and Frances would become her steady allies, fully supporting her work in the schools.

Alongside the support of her family Nano was blessed with her staunchest of allies – her Uncle Joseph, a barrister and man of great means but, as we have noted, 'the most disliked by the Protestants of any Catholic in the kingdom'. On becoming aware of Nano's courageous act in opening a school in Cove Lane, he encouraged her. His response by way of moral and financial support would enable Nano to put her enterprise on a firm foundation. In time to come it would serve to further her project beyond her hopes.

Her daring venture grew rapidly until Nano had five schools for girls, located across Cork City in Cove Lane, Philpot Lane, Shandon Street, Brown's Hill and at the junction of Cross Street and Sheares Street. Daily she would traverse the circuit from south to north, expending her fragile energies in a total and tireless manner. She said, 'I often think my schools will never bring me to heaven as I take only delight and pleasure in them'.

She laboured discreetly and alone, with only the assistance of the teachers whom she employed. Nano left the teaching of the three 'R's' to them, but the task of evangelisation and faith formation was her sole preserve. Daily she instructed the children and prepared them twice yearly for the sacraments. At the request of her brother and sister-in-law and with their financial support, she set up two schools for boys. The term 'faith formation' was not yet in vogue, but here again we get an insight into her forward thinking. Her dream of service also had a global dimension and with this in view she prepared some pupils to act as catechists in the West Indies. In a letter written in 1770 she wrote: 'I am sending boys to the West Indies. Some charitable men put themselves to a great expense for no other motive'. In the same letter, she continued: 'All my children are brought up to be fond of instructing as I think it lies in the power of the poor to be of more service that way than the rich'.

LANTERN WORK

Nano's vision of education was not restricted to children but also embraced adults. As we have noted, each evening she continued what would later be termed her 'lantern work'. She could be seen, clutching her lantern after the long day in the school, visiting the slums. Having served their needs and offered hope and light to them, she would silently return to her humble abode, where she contemplated and prayed over the encounters of her day. There in the company of Jesus, the Word made Flesh, she prayed for those she had encountered. In each she saw the face of Christ: he beckoned to her in the winding lanes. As we said earlier, his words must had a deep resonance for he: 'I was hungry, lonely, poor, imprisoned ... and you visited me' (Matthew 25:35–36). The destitute, the widowed, women of low repute – all were inside the circle of God's love and compassion, and similarly of hers.

Always there was the risk of discovery by the forces of the Crown. She describes how 'she took in the children by degrees' to avoid drawing any unwelcome publicity. Equally the daily immersion in the poverty of those she served left her own health at constant risk, and she was only too aware of the threat to her life in a lawless and violent city. So, she joyfully expended her wealth, health and strength in the schools, slums and attics of Cork city.

At a time when the role of women was largely subservient and restricted, Nano Nagle was a politically active woman. Her vision, courage, commitment and action worked to subvert more than a century of unjust oppression and denial of human rights. She continued this mission against all the hostility and resistance which came her way. Prophetic, pioneering, and courageous, she was a beacon of light and hope for those long held in the throes of despair and hopelessness.

FOR PONDERING

Dr Coppinger's panegyric on her death in 1784 reveals her tenacity of spirit: 'How often we have seen her, after a well spent day, returning through the darkness of the night, dripping with rain, mingling in the bustling crowd, moving thoughtfully along by the faint glimmering of a wretched lantern, withholding from herself in this manner the necessities of life to administer the comforts of it to others'.

What helps to keep me going when life is difficult?

CHAPTER 5
THE FOUNDATION OF THE PRESENTATION SISTERS

Presentation Sisters

By 1768 the years of daily toil were taking their toll on Nano's health, and ever a practical woman she was keen to ensure the permanence of her schools after her death. She turned once again to France to enlist the help of the Ursuline Congregation. But the labour involved was woven with threads of stress, strain and disappointment, as can be sensed in her letter written in 1769–1770 to Eleanor Fitzsimons, then a novice in the Ursuline Convent in France. While only a handful of Nano's letters are extant, they afford us glimpses both of a daring and passionate woman but also one who experienced vexation and frustration when her plans were being thwarted.

Throughout the entire endeavour to establish the Ursulines in Ireland, Nano was blessed with the steady collaboration both of Fr Francis Moylan, then Vicar General of the Diocese of Cork and his uncle, Patrick Doran, 'a learned and holy Jesuit'. The latter had returned to Cork following the suppression of the Jesuits in France in 1763. Both men supported and worked tirelessly with her to ensure the permanence of her work. Four years after Nano's death, Fr Moylan wrote: 'She prudently foresaw... that a work of this extensive charity could not long subsist, unless the persons charged with the Instruction considered it as a duty and attend to it, not for a salary, but from motives of religion and zeal for God's glory'.

A SHATTERED DREAM

On 9 May 1771, after many toils and tribulations the four Irish women trained in France arrived in Cork for the first foundation of the Ursulines in Ireland. Nano Nagle was named as the foundress. Since the convent she was building for them was not yet completed, they initially shared her humble cottage. Finally on 18 September 1771, the Sisters took formal possession of the Convent which Nano had built for them. One can only contemplate the sense of joy that must have filled her heart, now seeing her dream finally realised.

While much effort, planning and finance had gone into having all in readiness for the new foundation, Nano's joy in their arrival would prove to be short-lived. Her dream and hope of finally having a secure foothold into the future was shattered by the Catholic Church's long-standing law of enclosure.

The *Ursuline Annals* state: 'The Ursulines were bound by their Constitutions to enclosure and to the education of the higher orders of society, consequently could not, as she wished, visit the poor and the sick abroad nor devote themselves solely to the education of the poor at home'. Nano's schools were located in different parts of the city, and so they would be out of bounds for the Sisters. She had been naive in thinking that the rule of enclosure would not pertain when they came to Ireland.

She had hoped that when they finally came, these Sisters would do as she had been doing – walk the daily circuit to the schools; visit the hovels and the destitute. In a word, she needed women who would work on the streets and there encounter the Word made Flesh. For five years she had laboured in planning, writing, financing, building and praying for their arrival. Now her dream had faded like the morning mist. How can one ever comprehend the enormous cost of this grave disappointment to Nano? What was to be the future of her schools? Her health was deteriorating, her finances were depleted. Who or what would sustain her now in this darkest of hours?

GOD WAS HER GPS

For Nano in times of trial, tribulations and suffering, the one she addressed as 'The Almighty' was her lodestar. Now in this time of shadow and darkness she steadily turned her gaze to God. Rising early each morning to pray and again before retiring each evening, she inclined the ear of her heart, yearning to pick up the heartbeat of Christ. There she remained, watching and waiting with unshakeable faith. She contemplated the life of Jesus and placed all her confidence in him who had also known the shattering of his life's dream. He and none other could guide her path and give her the wisdom, guidance and discernment she now needed to take the next step. Only a person rooted firmly in God's love could write as she did with such breath-taking conviction: 'It is a good sign of our future success, to meet with crosses in the beginning'.

KEEPING WATCH

This period of her life had all the hallmarks of a dark night. It was a time when she was called to watch, to wait and to outstare the darkness. In the words of Edwina Gately 'There you prayed, Nano, hour after hour, the pain of your sickened body eclipsed by the ardent passion of the great Love Conspiracy that kept your soul shining in the darkness – sole witness to your whisper: "The Almighty is all-sufficient ... "'. She searched the divine horizons and kept faith with God's protective presence, seeking for the light of the Spirit to illuminate and guide her way.

Nano was being drawn deeply into the Passion of Christ. The words of Pope Francis mirror well what centuries earlier Nano Nagle must have come to know: 'When the Lord bestows a mission he always employs a process of purification, a process of perception, a process of obedience, a process of prayer'. Up to this moment, Nano had fearlessly taken the courageous steps of opening her schools and bringing the Ursulines to Ireland. Now at the age of fifty-seven one further fearless and courageous stepping out was required of her.

BEGIN AGAIN

In our later years who wants to make new beginnings? Yet out of the ashes of disquiet and disappointment Nano Nagle found a new fire urging her on, kindled by an increasing love for the poor. She set about taking her bravest step of all, which would have consequences far beyond Ireland and ensure that her life and legacy would be carried into the future.

She needed the hearts and hands of other generous women who would share in her passion for Christ and the despised of humankind. The *Annals* of South Presentation Convent Cork record that milestone when the seed of the Presentation Congregation was sown: 'Her heart was centered on the poor; her whole aim was to reform them. This was her object, her most ardent desire'. She sought to create a band of women filled with zeal and 'fired with Love's urgent longing' who would spend themselves and their entire life for the poor. She also wanted them not bound by the rule of enclosure but free to work on the streets of Cork, visit the workhouse, the hovels and attics of her day.

THE NEW CONGREGATION

She invited two of her helpers, Elizabeth Bourke and Mary Fouhy to share her poor residence in Cove Lane. There with these two companions she waited a further year for another helper to join them – Mary Anne Collins. With her arrival all was ready. On 24 December 1775, Nano and her three companions began the formal preparation required for taking religious vows on 24 June 1776. Nano chose St John of God as a religious name; his life had inspired her. In the fifteenth century, he had spent himself for the poor.

The following year, 24 June 1777, in the presence of Dr John Butler, Bishop of Cork, they made their profession of vows. The initial name of the foundation was 'The Society of the Charitable Instruction of the Sacred Heart of Jesus'. The title Nano chose was significant. This was the period when Jansenism was emphasising the divinity of Jesus to the eclipse of his humanity. In choosing this title for her new congregation Nano offers a window into her own theology and spirituality. She had a deep commitment to the mystery of the Incarnation, to the humanity of Jesus and his love for the poor and needy. These would be core values of her new foundation. In their lives of consecrated service, her sisters would seek to be the eyes, ears, hands and heart of the Word made Flesh in their service of the poor of Cork city. Of course, they too would become bound by enclosure, but the schools would be built within the convent grounds.

How did Nano mark the new foundation? She and her companions welcomed fifty beggars to dinner on Christmas Day 1777. Modelling their lives on that of the gospel Jesus she and her companions waited on them with profound reverence and joy. This tradition continued annually until 1887.

FOR PONDERING

In the face of adversity Nano wrote: 'You must think the Almighty permits everything for the best. You will see with His assistance, everything promises well'.

From the ashes and disappointments of your life, where did you draw the courage to begin again?

CHAPTER 6
ONGOING CHALLENGES
AND FINAL YEARS

The responsibilities of the fledgling congregation added to Nano's already heavy workload. There was the matter of building a new convent and financing it, the crafting for the congregation of a constitution that would embody her apostolic vision, and the selection of prospective candidates. She had a further desire to establish a home for 'aged and destitute women' and the plight of Cork's prostitutes was equally close to her heart.

Nano showed no signs of shrinking from the new challenges. Zeal and trust in Divine Providence were virtues embodied in her, and also required of those who would be her companions. She wrote, 'I can't too much admire your zeal and great trust in Divine Providence which I always looked on as the most settled beginning any foundation of this kind could have'. As she moved into the final years of her life, she would rely heavily on both.

Over the years Nano had developed a steady rhythm to her day of prayer and work. For her new congregation the self-same standards of prayer and of commitment to the apostolate would be integral. She had divested herself of all semblances of comfort and ease and lived an austere life. Let the words of the Annalist once more paint a picture of the standards she set: 'This was the road pointed out by Miss Nagle to be trodden by members of her congregation. She walked in it herself, her example traced the way to them, and they faithfully followed it. She was of a disposition most particularly austere. She never spared herself and she exacted from her associates all those practices of self-denial which she so nonchalantly imposed upon herself. Their meals were mean and frugal; and poor and comfortless as they were, no sooner were they ended than they were obliged to repair to their schools'.

Each of her sisters was dressed in 'a black gown plainly made, without fashion, over it a black handkerchief cross in front, a plain cap, a broad black ribbon bound tightly about the head. When going out to schools they wore the long cloaks, the hoods of which they always threw over the small black bonnet'.

INFECTIOUS INSPIRATION

Teresa Mulally, a milliner from Dublin inspired by Nano's work in Cork, felt called to similar work in Dublin. They became kindred spirits and corresponded from 1776–1783, the year prior to Nano's death. Teresa longed for the time when Nano would be in a position to respond to her request and send sisters to work in Dublin. In the company of a companion Teresa had visited Nano Nagle in Cork, and her companion painted a revealing picture of the encounter between these two valiant women. 'There entered a little elderly woman with a shabby silk cloak, an old hat turned up, a soiled dark cotton gown and a coarse black petticoat drabbled half-way and dripping wet, for it had rained heavily. When she announced her name to be Nagle, they embraced for the first time with hearts congenial … I asked her was she not afraid of taking a cold. "No," she replied, "I was susceptible enough of it but now I feel nothing". It really confounded me to see myself with a trunk of gay things, when a woman of ample fortune made such a humble appearance.'

SUFFERING IN MANY GUISES

These final years of Nano's life were marked with suffering in many guises. The failure of the Ursuline project had led to great disappointment. She was in financial distress with no money to finance any other foundation. Possessed of a deep spirit of poverty, a poverty that was the fruit of her many hours of contemplation of Jesus, she wrote to Teresa Mulally with exquisite simplicity: 'I am often without money, yet as everybody knows me, I don't mind it'. She was reduced to questing for alms not only on behalf of the schools, but also for disconsolate widows, orphans, reduced housekeepers and superannuated tradesmen. The *South Presentation Annals* record an incident when Nano was direly in need of funds, and offers us a vignette of her calibre, tenacity and patience. In a certain shop, where

Nano in contemplation

previously she had received alms, she was rebuffed and discourteously treated by one of the assistants. For two hours, sitting on a bundle of skins, she waited patiently for the owner. On his arrival he was informed of the importunity of the old mendicant. When he saw who she was he was deeply disturbed, for above all others he most venerated her. In the words of T J Walsh: 'Nano's purchase was eighteenth century Cork with its meat shambles, its stampeding cattle, its salt cellars, its fetor, its press gangs, its faction fights, and its hoards of illiterate children'.

During the final year of her life, 1784, Nano's deteriorating health was evident to those around her. Her lungs were diseased with tuberculosis, her feet ulcerated. But she lived to the end an austere life of penance and fasting, about which her sisters were obliged to secrecy. 'In every step of her wounded feet she pleaded for the poor.' She continued her daily circuit with the aid of her walking stick. On Monday and Tuesday 5 and 6 April Nano visited her schools, where she read the account of the Passion of Jesus three times. She did not feel any fatigue, but remarked, 'and you know it is pretty long'. On Holy Thursday night she remained kneeling in vigil for eleven hours in adoration of her Lord. Easter Sunday was celebrated on 11 April.

Tuesday 20 April, six days before her death, it rained very heavily and Nano got drenched. The following morning as she made her way to school she was afflicted with a haemorrhage, 'at a lady's house' near her school at Cross Street. It would seem that lady was well acquainted with Nano and begged her to go no further but to return home. Nano replied 'What a coward you are! I have a mind to go to the schools and walk it off as I am used to do'. But on this occasion she couldn't walk it off: instead she got a weakness there and then. When she recovered 'the dear woman walked her home for the last time'.

By this time an inflammation had formed in her lungs. She suffered with a violent cough, and was very weak. The doctor ordered her to be blistered but Nano was aware that she was in grave danger and that a cure was impossible At her bedside as she lay dying, 'her afflicted community assembled around her' – this handful of faithful followers

– 'learning from her how to die as they had learned from her example how they should live'. She bequeathed to them her spiritual legacy: 'Love one another as you have hitherto done'. She entrusted this fragile group of companions to the care of Sr Angela Collins, urging her to be kind and vigilant to the community now committed to her care. She died on the morning of Monday 26 April 1784, aged sixty-five years. Her wish was to be buried in the public cemetery, and so share the common lot of the poor. The Ursulines were deeply opposed to this and instead asked that Nano and her Sisters be buried in the Ursuline cemetery.

FOR PONDERING

> *In regard to preparing for death, Henri Nouwen wrote: 'The central question is not, "How much time remains?" but rather, "How can we prepare so that our dying will be a new way for us to send our spirit and God's spirit to those whom we have loved and who have loved us?"'*

After your death, how would you like to be remembered?

CHAPTER 7
NANO'S SPIRITUALITY

It is time now to look more closely at what we would now call Nano's spirituality. The word itself can be daunting and off-putting: it seems to refer to a rarefied phenomenon, the concern solely of those in the cloister or monastery, but not for ordinary mortals whose lives are immersed in the marketplace. However, writer Richard Rohr challenges this assumption. His invitation to us is, 'Get in on the big and hidden secret: God seeks and desires intimacy with me. Then everything changes'. Christian spirituality means the quest for God, attentiveness to the Holy Spirit and openness to the person of Jesus Christ. We each have an open invitation to join the Divine Family, to come right in, to share in the very life of God, to live deeply connected to the Divine. We are invited to live in the marketplace with intention, attention, in healthy relationship with ourselves, others, the world and God. Attentive listening to this invitation leads us into a gospel-oriented spirituality.

LOVE CHANGES EVERYTHING

So it was for Nano Nagle, when she surrendered herself to God's alluring and steadfast love. Everything changed for her; how she lived and how she died. God's allurement brought her right in on the big and hidden secret. She experienced in a radical way God's desire for intimacy with her and responded fully. She became a captive flame – a woman ablaze with love. In her daily rhythm of spiritual practice she began by dipping the wick of her life into the oil of Divine Love. Each evening after her long day's work she returned to be with her Tremendous Lover, carrying in her heart and mind the grief, pain and needs of those she had encountered during the day. Her spirituality held no dualism. 'The more she moved among the people, especially the poor, the more she was drawn to prayer and mystical union with God, the source of her energy and her mission.'

Bishop Coppinger wrote: 'At Chapel every day, from five o'clock in the morning until nine, and during the Divine Sacrifice, how unaffected her appearance – silent, motionless, absorbed in recollection ... Her evening devotions were as regularly prolonged in the same unaltered posture!'

NANO, ICON OF GOD'S COMPASSION

Reflecting on the encounter with God in prayer Daniel O' Leary wrote: 'God wants us to sit for him, not that he may paint our portrait but that he may paint his own within us'. In prayer the Divine Artist gazes on us with love and seeks to draw us into a profound encounter that results in a gradual capturing of our entire being. Nano took her place on the watch tower, watching and waiting for the Lord to reveal his ways to her. As she waited her gaze gradually became clearer and more penetrating. She received light for each step of her journey and for each of her decisions. As Pope Francis urges us to do, she stood at the threshold, the place where the Spirit groans aloud: there where we no longer know what to say, nor what to expect, but where the Spirit knows the plans of God.

NANO NAGLE ICON

To mark the bi-centenary of the death of Nano Nagle in 1984, artist Desmond Kyne was commissioned by the

Presentation Congregation to create in an icon a fitting memento of her life. This icon can be contemplated at the centre in Ballygriffin, Nano's birthplace, and also at St Finbarr's South Parish Church in Cork city. The artist drew on the medium of kinetic stained glass to create an icon which evokes an inspirational story of the faith, courage and heroic leadership of a singular, purposeful woman, whose entire life was focused on God and God's people. Her passion and commitment for the Gospel glows through each detail of the work and reflects the spirituality that fired her life and mission.

HEART SPEAKS TO HEART

In the icon the image of the Sacred Heart is emblazoned like a jewel on Nano's gown, with a symbol of the Cross. Devotion to the Sacred Heart was popular in her day, and was central to her spirituality as we have seen. Her great enterprise had been firmly rooted and held in a love that was both human and divine, whence she became a living icon of the compassionate heart of Jesus to the hungry poor of Cork.

The centrality of her prayer emanates from the icon. Over a lifetime, God had painted His portrait in her. The Incarnate Love of the Gospel Jesus, daily contemplated, propelled her to his service.

Nano contemplated in stillness the fact that in Jesus the Word had become flesh and embraced our human condition. He was vulnerable, wounded, rejected, and paid the ultimate price of self-donating love. Once Nano was awakened to this mystery of Incarnation, she moved to act with the self-same justice, to love the needy tenderly, and to walk humbly among them. One imagines her before the tabernacle, leaning into the heart of Christ as she whispers, 'What should I do? How do you wish me to play my part in healing this corner of the fractured and broken world?' As we have seen earlier her response took different turns, until finally she found the direction that was meant for her. Caught by the passionate love of Jesus she and subsequently her companions were drawn to move from 'the temple of riches to the tables of the poor'. In the middle panel of the icon the Lamb of God is at the centre of a small group of poor children: innocence and love are partners in suffering.

THE EUCHARIST

Another central component of Nano Nagle's spirituality was the Eucharist. In silent adoration she pondered the mystery of love outpoured on her and on the world. Jesus, her Lord and Master, had become a suffering servant, and she pondered his words, 'I have given you an example, so that you may copy what I have done' (John 13:15). For Nano, the celebration of the Eucharist was not some private devotion, disconnected from her life's enterprise. Taking seriously the injunction given by Jesus, 'Do this in memory of me' she gave all she had in loving service of God's people. In the words of Astrid Lobo Gajiwala 'Nano presided at life's Eucharistic banquet'. She became a living Eucharist: like the bread in Jesus' hands, she too was taken, blessed, broken, and given over to those who needed sustenance.

LIFE POURED OUT

The gospel account of the woman pouring out the alabaster jar of costly perfume on Jesus' feet (Luke 7:36–50) captures well Nano's life of self-donation to the poor. Instead of hoarding her gifts and sealing herself against the cry of God's poor, she shares with them her power, position, and prosperity. Aided by the light of a lantern flame and her walking stick, this frail woman walked Cork's grubby, muddied, smelly laneways in compassionate loving service daily. Fortified by her spiritual practices, she became love poured out for the world.

HANDS

The icon presents Nano gazing outward onto the world. Her right hand rests in stillness and quiet, while the left hints at a movement towards action. It suggests a woman who holds as important the need to reflect and discern the insights birthed in her as she prays. She brought her life into her prayer – the encounters, struggles, difficulties she experienced. She sought the guiding hand of the good Spirit to enable her to make radical choices, confident that God was with her. The wellspring of her ministry flowed out from her deep awareness of God at work in her life. Her response to him had but one desire, to give him honour and glory. In a letter to Teresa Mulally in 1779 she wrote, 'I hope that the Almighty will direct you to what is most to his honour and glory'.

SHARING THE PASCHAL MYSTERY

The Passion of Christ was ever central to those long hours of prayer. Writer Ilia Delio comments: 'To find oneself in the mirror of the cross is to see the world not from the foot of the cross but from the cross itself. How we see is how we love, and what we love is what we become'. In the icon the love and support of the Father is revealed to Nano through the image of the arm of Christ, which envelops her in a protective and comforting way. His pierced hand indicates that he is familiar with suffering. She too will experience in her life that the dynamic of the cross is a core part of discipleship: not deliverance from suffering but the inner strength to endure it in a graced way. Earlier we referred to Nano's devotion to the Paschal Mystery, and how even in the final weeks of her life, in spite of her weakened state of health, she still went to the schools in Holy Week where she read the account of the Passion to her children.

Pierced hand

She experienced at first-hand the 'wood of the cross' in her own life and ministry. From the beginning of her commitment to Cork in 1754 until her death in 1784, her journey was marked by trials, suffering, rejection, misunderstanding, scorn and derision. She was familiar with grief, loss, sickness, helplessness, failure and disappointments. Dr Coppinger has left a description of the manner in which Nano suffered: 'She has been bitterly cursed in our streets as a mere imposter; she has been charged with having squandered her money upon the building of houses for the sole purpose of getting a name, and with deceiving the world with her throng of beggars' brats. Has it not even been said that her schools were a seminary for prostitution?'

She embraced the Cross in whatever way it visited her and endured it with love and faith. In time she experienced its transformative effects in her life and living. A few quotations from one of her letters give us a glimpse of her faith and confidence in the Almighty in such times:

'The best works meet with the greatest crosses' and 'I must say, every disadvantage that I had, the Almighty has been pleased to turn to our advantage'. 'You must think the Almighty permits everything for the best. You will see with his assistance, everything promises well.'

HER SECRET SCRIPTURES

As a Presentation sister and follower of Nano Nagle, one of my deepest regrets is the lack of original material from this wonderful woman. We know but a little of her secret scriptures: only sixteen of her letters are extant. What is evident is that once she was 'resigned to the Divine Will' she embarked on a journey that, left to her own devices, she could never have scripted. God became the main author of her life and she collaborated fully with him. In his eulogy on the life and work of Nano Nagle, Bishop Coppinger gathered it up in one phrase: 'The Almighty presided at the counsels of her heart'.

FOR PONDERING

Nano Nagle was an authentic woman, who lived the mysticism of service. 'Her feet bore the sores of a pilgrim on a journey with a cold shivering humanity and that is where she walked into Christ, and together, step by struggling footstep they forged a new path into new life.'

How would it be if God were to preside at the counsels of your heart?

CHAPTER 8
NANO'S PROPHETIC VOICE

In 2015 Pope Francis wrote a letter on Consecrated Life, titled *Keep Watch*. He highlighted how the prophetic person is called to 'search the horizons of our life and our times, in watchful prayer; to peer into the night in order to recognise the fire that illuminates and guides ... to keep awake and watch ...'

Nano Nagle was a prophetic woman: the passionate love of God beckoned to her and she responded heroically.

In that spirit she set her face against the oppressive system of her day. Resolute in the conviction that she was being sent by God to the poor, she dared to risk all, unafraid of the consequences. She pioneered a socio-religious movement that drew her into communion with the shunned and poorest in society. She took her place alongside them in a ministry of service. Here she would encounter the broken body of Christ. Her mission was clear: to bind up their wounds, to heal the broken-hearted, to restore their sense of dignity, so that they would come to know they were the beloved of God. For Nano, nothing was more certain than that God was on the side of the poor and vulnerable: in God's eyes they were the important ones.

A PASSION FOR JUSTICE

Her prophetic and zealous stance and her creativity would in time help to lift the yoke of tyranny. Because of her the oppressed and marginalised would begin to raise their bowed heads and walk with dignity and hope. Dr

Coppinger offers an insight into the pain and anguish Nano experienced due to an impoverished teaching of the Faith by a weakened Church. The Penal Laws left people ignorant, over-burdened, devoid of any sense of their own worth and dignity before God. 'She felt the loss of many souls, a prey to the miseries of ignorance; she lamented the silence of these pulpits, where wisdom should have cried aloud, and zeal should have thundered with all its energy; she grieved to behold the tribunals of penances as cautiously concealed as the transgressions deposited in them: she was shocked to see the word of God chained down in injustice, and the little ones crying for this bread, while there were none to break it to them. With such incentives, no difficulties could deter her. She entered on the Great Work.'

ENLARGED HORIZONS

The Presentation Congregation Gathering 2012 described Nano Nagle as 'a heart-centred woman who immersed herself in the life of Jesus and in turn in the lives of the poor and marginalised of her day. Passion propelled her outward to be one with the poor and an ardent advocate on their behalf.' Those who truly follow her in her vision and her legacy are challenged 'to be immersed in the lives of poor and marginalized people, who open us to the Mystery of Love, and to be prophetic voices with them for the transformation of unjust systems locally and globally'.

Nano's conversion revealed both her deep social awareness and her social conscience. Seized by the light of God's truth, she could no longer conform to expected norms. She became a prophetic voice for her times.

POLITICAL DANGERS

Nano herself had daily lived with the awareness that severe punishment was her lot if she were to be apprehended for violating the Penal Laws. Like Dorothy Day in the twentieth century, referred to as 'the radical conscience of the American Church', or the Jewish convert Edith Stein, strong in the face of the Holocaust, or Joan of Arc who remained unyielding to churchmen who had her burned at the stake for obeying her conscience rather than them, she faced hostility and public ridicule, and yet remained undaunted by the fears that beset her. Her life mission had one unwavering purpose: love of the poor.

Her courageous and daring actions bore fruit in God's good time. Her pioneering of the education of the neediest would transform many lives. She was the first post-reformation Irish Founder and a beacon to future Irish women and men who would found teaching congregations, among them Bl. Edmund Rice (Christian Brothers, 1802), Bishop Daniel Delany (Brigidine Sisters, 1807), Mary Aikenhead (Sisters of Charity, 1815), Teresa Ball (Irish Loreto Sisters, 1821), Catherine McAuley (Sisters of Mercy, 1828) and Margaret Aylward (Sisters of the Holy Faith, 1867).

WHO WILL SPEAK IF YOU DON'T?

If Nano were walking our world today, what burning issues would drive her to a life of self-donation? Our global landscape reveals greed, abuse of power, unjust structures, and systems that leave the majority of people endlessly shackled. Do I see – as Nano saw – the face of Jesus Christ in the caravans of migrants who trek from one unwelcoming country to another or who travel by sea at the peril of their lives? Do I allow the unwanted of the earth to disturb my complacency or have I become numbed? The Lord hears the cry of the poor: do I?

Jesus didn't merely decry the systemic injustices of his time. He did something: he denounced all forms of domination by human beings over one another and witnessed to the dignity of every person on the planet. Nano played her part, and now it is my turn. Our world today urgently needs prophetic voices who can by actions and advocacy bring hope to those 'who sit in darkness and the shadow of death' (Luke 2:79). Who will speak if I don't?

Pope Francis puts the challenge trenchantly: 'Prophecy is born whenever we allow ourselves to be challenged by God, not when we are concerned to keep everything quiet and under control. Prophecy is not born from my thoughts, from my closed heart. When the Gospel overturns certainties, prophecy arises. Only someone who is open to God's surprises can become a prophet …We need lives that show the miracle of God's love. Today we need prophecy, but real prophecy: not fast talkers who promise the impossible, but persons who give testimony that the Gospel is possible'.

FOR PONDERING

Edwina Gately paints a stark picture of the prophet: 'Prophets do not conform. They burst upon our flat horizon with creative alternatives and new models of being human'.

Who are the prophets of today who inspire and challenge me?

CHAPTER 9
NANO'S LEGACY

In her book *Nano Nagle: Woman of the Gospel*, Sr Mary Pius O'Farrell includes a eulogy to Nano attributed to Sr Ursula Kavanagh: 'What will become of the innocent orphans, hundreds of whom she drew from vice and ignorance? What will become of the sick, naked and afflicted whom she so often relieved and comforted with her unbounded charities? The object of her greatest distress was that of her greatest compassion, without being confined to any religion'. Nano Nagle is not a figure confined to the past but someone whose vision is as relevant today as it was in her own time. As Jesus says: 'The poor you will always have with you' (John 12:8).

SR ANGELA COLLINS

Nano's life and vision sparked an answering fire in the hearts of her first companions. On her deathbed she entrusted to Mary Ann Collins, known as Sr Angela, her handful of faithful followers, and tasked them with continuing her mission. The *South Presentation Annals* record that 'She then gave up her charge of superioress into the hands of Sr. Angela Collins, recommending her to be vigilant; to be kind to those whom she committed to her care; and by her efforts to ensure as much as possible the continuation of the good work she had only begun, and the progress of which she was not worthy to see'.

The *Annals* continue: 'She merely wished them to become as she herself was, the servants of the Poor ... This was the road pointed out by Miss Nagle, to be trodden by the members of her Congregation – she walked in it herself

– her example traced the way to them and they faithfully followed it'.

Sr Angela embraced with rocklike courage and fidelity the mantle of leadership entrusted to her. One cannot but be moved to profound gratitude and amazement at how she embraced and led this fragile, fledgling community for the next twenty years. In the years subsequent to Nano's death in 1784 the very survival of the enterprise was threatened through sickness, death and the withdrawal of some members. Sr Angela steered her little group of sisters through these difficult times. They endured great poverty, privations and near destitution as a consequence of misappropriation of resources and betrayal of trust by financial advisors. What courage, faith and zeal were required of her in such times! Did she draw strength from Nano in this lean and bleak period when it seemed that her little congregation was in danger of extinction? Did Nano's own words, written to her friend in Dublin, Teresa Mulally, in 1783 sustain her, and give her courage to take the next step, when sometimes that must have been all she could manage to do? 'The best works meet with the greatest crosses. I don't approve of your desponding so much as I perceived in your last letter. Though neither you nor I should live to see the Congregation prosper in our time, yet I hope that it may prosper hereafter and be of universal service to the Kingdom.'

Raphael Consedine refers to Sr Angela as a woman 'whose contribution was essentially personal and in the order of faith … without her fidelity, Nano's Institute would almost certainly have perished within a year of her death. When humanly speaking there was nothing to hope for, Mary Ann Collins listened, not to the dictates of self-interest but to the Divine Call in her life. In so doing, she gave to the Institute an example of single-hearted faithfulness which both captured the past shared with Nano and pointed the way to the future for those who came to join her'. In spite of a precarious struggle for survival, the seeds of new hope gradually emerged with an increase of members and approval of new constitutions in 1791. These were drafted by Fr Laurence Callanan OFM. in Cork, who had been Nano's spiritual director. Aware of her devotion to the feast of Mary's Presentation in the Temple, he agreed with the Sisters to change the title of the congregation to Sisters of the Presentation of the Blessed Virgin Mary.

A RICH LEGACY

Moses never entered the Promised Land, and Nano's cherished hope and global vision for mission began to flower only after her death. Presentation history evolved as each new call was answered. This booklet does not allow for a detailed account of each foundation, but let us sketch the dynamic energy and courage of those early women, who, fired by the self-same spirit of Nano, and filled with Nano's zeal and vision, travelled to the peripheries of the earth in response to repeated appeals to be in solidarity with the caravan of God's people. 'They were women of listening hearts. To them the Spirit spoke: Come! So they rose up to follow'.

EARLY FOUNDATIONS & OVERSEAS EXPANSION

Within two decades of Nano' death, five foundations had been established in Ireland: Killarney (1793), George's Hill, Dublin (1794), Waterford (1798), North Presentation,

Cork (1799) and Kilkenny (1800). This is testament to the dynamic energy of the spirit and the readiness of these women to respond.

Overseas expansion began in 1833 with a foundation in Newfoundland. Nano's vision of service to the world had begun. This expansion has continued, such that Presentation Sisters are now to be found across the globe. Pioneering women left the safety of the known and went forth carrying the flame of the gospel to England, America and Australia, and to Asia, Africa, Latin America, Eastern Europe and the Holy Land. The number of native-born sisters continues to increase today. Could Nano ever have dreamed how far flung would be the impact of her life? As the hymn has it: 'I am standing on the shoulders of the ones who came before me. I am honoured by their passion for our liberty. I will stand a little taller, I will work a little longer, and my shoulders will be there to hold the ones who follow me'.

UNIQUE AND UNREPEATABLE

Nano Nagle was a prophet of love. We have noted that her dying words were 'Love one another as you have hitherto done'. Across the globe today the charism of Nano Nagle, to be love in the world, is cherished by a strong network of sisters, colleagues, associates, students and friends of Nano – the entire Presentation Family. With commitment and creative imagination, they seek to find an entry point in human life where they can make a difference. They identify systemic injustice and its causes and seek to listen to the cry of the earth and the poor. No effort is spared to raise awareness of the burning issues of today's world. They work and collaborate with likeminded groups in beaming the lantern flame of hope and transformation across geographical, political and cultural borders. By being collaborators with God in the care of humanity and our Earth, they make the gospel vision a reality as they place themselves daily in the path of the poorest of the poor. Nano Nagle bids us to move from our safe and comfortable nests, from our self-isolation and complacency, and to move to the peripheries, to life on the razor's edge. She wouldn't want us to simply replicate her life but to seek new pathways, new strategies, imaginative responses, that act as a counterpoint in a world that has largely lost its moral compass.

Tucked away in Pope St John Paul's 1989 document on the Laity are the arresting words: 'each Christian as an individual is unique and irrepeatable'. What wonderful Good News: I am personally called by God. God counts on me! I matter to God. I am invited to join in the great work of love, to make a difference: 'You go into my vineyard too' (see Matthew 20:1–16). What will my response be?

There is a common saying among Hispanic people: *Dios te puso en mi camino* – 'God has put you in my path'. God put Nano Nagle in the path of the poor of Cork and they in turn were put in her path and changed her. We can search for God in the heavens and fail to recognise his face when he comes to us disguised as people. We should not underestimate the importance a single person can have. There are many examples in Scripture where someone strolls across the stage of salvation history, delivers their short message, and in that brief encounter, and unknowingly, is a messenger of the divine to another. However insignificant we may consider ourselves, in the eyes of God we are each his chosen instruments.

ROLE MODELS

The words of the army official cited earlier bear repeating: 'What the world needs is more Nano's'. Role models are pathfinders and trailblazers. They inspire us, widen the horizons of our lives, and help us to dare believe that we are capable of great things. They raise our ideals and call forth the best in us.

ARTISANS OF A NEW HUMANITY

In the Sermon on the Mount, Jesus is inviting us to make a difference in our world by being agents of change. Gandhi puts it sharply: 'Be the change you want to happen'. Nano can help us here: she would understand our sense of feeling overwhelmed and inadequate before the political, economic, and social systems in our world today. But she would remind us that 'the Almighty makes use of the weakest means to bring about his work'. So, she would have us trust in the power of the Spirit and set our faces to the wind, trusting that in the economy of the kingdom of God our handful of tiny seeds will thrive and sprout and give shelter to those who need it (see Matthew 13:31–32).

She would advise us that if we are to be witnesses to divine values in an uncaring world, we need to keep close to God in prayer and to live out of Jesus' call to the disciples during the storm at sea: 'Do not be afraid: it is I' (John 6:20). It helps to know that this call, 'Do not be afraid' recurs some 140 times in the Bible: obviously God knows that we humans are easily daunted by things we cannot manage!

To be disciples means that we put our feet in the footsteps of Jesus. Living by gospel values, we do what we can to help in the liberation of those dominated by the forces of oppression; we live simply and sustainably, work for peace and justice and for the integrity of creation. As Pope Francis says, we are to be light bearers as we try to live through love with one another:

'Today, when the networks of human communication have made unprecedented advances, we share the challenge of finding and sharing a 'mystique' of living together, of mingling and encounter, of embracing and supporting one another, of stepping into this flood tide which, while chaotic, can become a genuine experience of fraternity, a caravan of solidarity, a sacred pilgrimage.' (*Evangelii Gaudium*, 87)

FOR PONDERING

'We all exist only for this – to be the human place God has chosen for his presence, his manifestation, his epiphany' (Thomas Merton). We are carriers of God's dream, unique and irrepeatable for every living being, for the fertile earth and for the mysterious universe.

How does this statement touch my heart?

FURTHER READING

You are welcome to visit both the birthplace of Nano Nagle at Ballygriffin, Co. Cork and her tomb at Nano Nagle Place, Douglas Street, Cork city.

BIBLIOGRAPHY

Consedine, Raphael. *Listening Journey: A Study of the Spirit and Ideals of Nano Nagle and the Presentation Sisters* (Congregation of Presentation Sisters, 1986).

Coppinger, William. *Life of Nano Nagle* (1794).

Flanagan, O'Brien, and O'Leary (eds). *Nano Nagle and an Evolving Charism: A Guide to Educators, Leaders and Care Providers* (Dublin: Veritas, 2017).

Hartnett, Kieran. *Nano Nagle: Woman of Vision* (1975).

Nagle, Nano. 'Letters of Nano Nagle' (Presentation Sisters Union, 2020). http://pbvm.org/wp-content/uploads/2020/06/Letters-of-Nano-Nagle-151305-1.pdf.

O'Farrell, Mary Pius. *Nano Nagle: Woman of the Gospels* (Cork: Cork Publishing Ltd, 1996).

Raftery, Deirdre, with Catriona Delaney and Catherine Nowlan-Roebuck. *Nano Nagle: The Life and Legacy* (Dublin: Irish Academic Press, 2018).

Walsh, T J. *Nano Nagle and the Presentation Sisters* (Dublin: Gill, 1959).

PRESENTATION WEBSITES

International Presentation Association, http://internationalpresentationassociation.org.

Nano Nagle Birthplace Ballygriffin, Ireland, www.nanonaglebirthplace.ie.

Nano Nagle Place, https://nanonagleplace.ie.

Nano Nagle Resources, www.nanonagle.org.

Presentation Sisters, Ireland South West Province, http://presentationsisterssw.ie.

Presentation Sisters, Ireland North East Province, https://presentationsistersne.ie.

Union of the Sisters of the Presentation of the Blessed Virgin Mary, www.pbvm.org.

Prayer for the Beatification of Venerable Nano Nagle

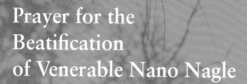

O God,
who enkindled in the heart of
   your servant, Nano Nagle,
the fire of your love,
and a consuming desire to serve
   You in any part of the world,
grant that we also may love You,
   and make you much loved.
And if it be for the glory of God,
   and the salvation of souls,
grant that soon she may be raised
   to the altars of your Church.
Through Christ our Lord.
Amen.